# POEMS COMPILED

## A Lifetime's Collection

### ADRIENNE WILLIS

WestBow
PRESS
A DIVISION OF THOMAS NELSON

WestBow Press books may be ordered through booksellers or by contacting:

WestBow Press
A Division of Thomas Nelson
1663 Liberty Drive
Bloomington, IN 47403
www.westbowpress.com
1-(866) 928-1240

ISBN: 978-1-4497-6775-4 (sc)

Library of Congress Control Number: 2012917798

Printed in the United States of America

WestBow Press rev. date: 10/04/2012

This book is lovingly dedicated to:

My mother, Juanita Eleanor Martin, who
first got me interested in books.

Mrs. Beverly Wooten, who gave me a subscription to
*Ranger Rick*, which increased my interest in nature.

The GOD Who created me, gave me my
talents and Who has always been with me.

# Contents

## Psalms

## Insights

## Essays

# INTRODUCTION

*Poems Compiled* is a collection of various poems and essays that I have written over the years, from Grade School until recently. At the risk of sounding vain, it's a compilation of my poetic creativity.

I've written many things over the years; poems, short stories, even some history manuscripts. But this will be my first published work. I've always wanted to be an author and I figured it was about time that I got something in print.

These works were written over a period of years and at different points in my life. I hope that those who read them will gain enjoyment and perhaps some inspiration.

# Part One:

# Poems

Part One is a collection of poems, most of which are about nature.

*A Rain Haiku* is the oldest poem I ever wrote; I made it in 1980 when I was eleven years old. I got the idea from reading the "Ink Links" section from the January issue of my *Ebony Jr.!* magazine. Technically, it's not a proper haiku, but I've been calling it that for this long, why stop now?

*Green* began in 1985 although it went through several renovations until it reached its current form in the 1990's.

The other poems were written in 1989 while I was a student at the University of Findlay. Each of them started out as an assignment in the poetry class I was taking at the time. *What is in Paradise?* was the first.

*A Squirrel # 3* has an interesting background. It was my third assignment for the poetry class. We were supposed to make what the teacher called a 'concrete' poem which, as I understood it, was a word drawing. I decided to write my poem about a squirrel and to literally draw a picture.

Well the teacher said that my drawing was nice, but that the words should have been emphasized more. So I wrote *A Squirrel*. I decided to include both in this book. This is compiled works after all.

*Rainbow in my Hand* is a recent poem showing how rainbows aren't always in the sky.

# POEMS

# A Rain Haiku

The gentle rain
fell from the sky
and gave water to the world.

# Green

Green is the freshness of a new season's taste,
Green is the scent of the March breeze in one's face.

Green is a color that soon spreads everywhere,
Green is the breaking of winter's bleak state.

Green is a sight without equal of peer,
Green is the sign that springtime is here.

Green is all of nature as it starts to grow and thrive,
When the season of death is over and everything comes alive.

# What is in Paradise?

What is in Paradise?
I'll say what is:

Bright light, clean air, blue skies
Pure lakes, rivers and streams
Stately mountains, rolling hills and straight paths
Green grass, tall trees and multicolored flowers
Friendly animals, loving people, mighty angels
God the Father, God the Son and God the Holy Spirit

What is in Paradise?
I'll say what's not:

Hate, violence, war
Filth, germs disease
Separation, tears, sorrow
Pain, death, fear
Cruelty, evil, sin

What is in Paradise?
I'll say what is:

Cleanliness, sweet fragrance, heavenly music
Beauty, perfection, fulfillment
Love, peace and fun

What is in Paradise?
I'll say what is:

Everlasting joy and gladness

# Red

What is red?

Fiery, hot flames
Strong, sturdy bricks
Heart shaped valentines
Maple leaves in autumn
Fresh crisp apples
Bright Christmas ribbons

Red is a beautiful color,
Totally unlike any other.

# A Squirrel
## # 3

Bushy tail for flicking and showing
Clever hands for digging and carrying
Agile body for climbing and scurrying
Sturdy legs for jumping
Hoarding nuts for eating

# Squirrel

Bushy, flickering tail
Agile, scurrying body

Leaping, jumping, climbing
Seeking, searching, finding

Picking, digging, carrying
Burying, storing, hoarding

# Stars

Look at the stars up in heaven so high,
All glowing and shining as they in their orbits swing by.

The Pleiades, Orion and countless others so bright,
Truly a dazzling and cosmic sight.

And they have a purpose those glowing points in the sky,
All so beautiful they make me want to cry.

Those celestial orbs that fill the sky with light,
Display the Lord's power and proclaim His might.

# Artificial Flowers

Flowers on the table.
Green stems, green leaves, yellow petals,
Beautiful!

Take a closer look…
Rooted not in dirt but plastic.

Closer still and touch…
Petals with no softness,
Hard dry stems with no moisture.

Come very close and take a whiff,
No sweet flower smell,
No fragrance at all.

Flowers on the table.
Beautiful.
Artificial.
A lie.

# Autumn

It's autumn and the time of death is fast approaching.

The days are growing steadily shorter.
The air ever more chilly.

The leaves are turning brown.
One by one they die and drop to the ground.
Their only lament is a crunching sound if feet tread on them.

The birds are flying away and taking with them their songs.
The animals are preparing to sleep or survive.

Soon all the trees will be naked and stark.
The fields will be barren.
The weather cold and harsh.
Life will be still.
Icy, snowy death will abound.

But do not be sad.

Spring will return.
The fields and the trees will once again turn green.
The weather will again become warm.
The animals and birds will be back.

Death will again be followed by life.

# Wolf Song

Off in the distance the wolf pack howls.
The night brothers have gathered together.
Hear their voices as they sing.

They sing a song sharp and clear.
They sing a song of mystery.
Hear the chorus as it reaches to the sky.

Hear the song of the wolf.

# Rainbow in my Hand

There's a rainbow in the sky;
And a rainbow in my hand.
Six colors in the air;
Six colors in a metal band.

Red: blazing fire,
Orange: the setting sun.
Yellow: the sun at its height,
Green: the grass beneath.
Blue: the midday sky,
Purple: a field of violets.

Ruby: blazing fire,
Garnet: the setting sun.
Gold: the sun at its height,
Emerald: the grass beneath.
Sapphire: the midday sky,
Amethyst: a field of flowers.

There's a rainbow in the sky;
And a rainbow in my hand.
Six colors in the air;
Six colors in a metal band.

# Part Two:

# God

Part two is a collection of works that deal with God; His qualities, who He is, what He Means to me and who I am to Him.

I got the idea for *Valentine* while I was in High School. It was Valentine's Day and it occurred to me that everyone was giving valentines to everyone. To everyone that is, except God. Valentine's Day is about love and since He is love shouldn't He get one too?

It was the same with *Friendship Day*. On that day we celebrate friends and He is my best friend.

*Outshines* was also written in High School.

*The One I Love* had its beginnings in my Findlay poetry class. We were supposed to use imagery and metaphors to describe a specific person. Guess Who this one is about?

*Beloved* was written while I was attending Messiah College from 1990-1993.

*Who I am* and *Not Disappointed* were written between 94-98. Those were pretty rough years for me. I was out of college but hadn't found steady employment, so I often felt like a failure. My mom told me that I should think positively about myself, affirm myself. So I wrote these poems trying to see myself as God sees me.

I don't remember when exactly I wrote *The God of So Much*; It was either in High School or college. I had always loved mythology and it struck me as funny that so many ancient cultures had had gods and spirits for every little thing; from the sun to the insects, to fire, and hunting. It made me realize how great the true God is, Who is in control over all of these things and so much more!

# GOD

# Valentine

Dearest Lord Jesus,
Your valentine to me was the cross.
My valentine to you is my life.

I love You

Happy Valentine's Day

# Friendship Day

Dearest Lord Jesus,

August 5th is Friendship Day and I just wanted to write a letter to You since You are my best friend.

Dear Lord, you've known and watched over me since my conception. You've protected me, guided me and most of all You've always been there for me.
When I need to talk You listen.
When I'm upset You always understand.

I know that You love me, Lord.
I want You to know that You are my dearest Friend and I love You more than my own life.

Happy Friendship Day

Your friend, Adrienne

# Outshines

As the sun outshines a candle,
So the Lord outshines all else,
And lights the way for those who trust Him.

As the moon reflects the sun,
So we as Christians should reflect Christ,
And honor Him in all we do.

# The One I Love

O Lord, You are clothed in beauty, glory and majesty.
Your smile is the sunshine lighting up the world.
Your voice is the sound of waves on the shore.
Your laughter is the loveliest of music.

Your footsteps are heralds of peace.
Your hands are instruments of healing.
Your mind is the source of wisdom.
Your heart is the wellspring from which all love flows.

Your arms are my safe haven.
By Your side is where I long to be.
Your love is my strength.
Your presence is the only place where there is joy.

You are a blanket giving warmth and security.
You are the rain giving freshness and life.
You are the sun giving light and hope.
You are all that was missing in my life before.

You are the One I love.

# My Beloved

I love You, Lord Jesus.

You are my Lord, my Savior, my Master, and my God.
My Father, my Brother, my Friend, and my Beloved.

You are my life,
Without You there is nothing.

You are my Beloved and my Friend.

I love You, Lord Jesus.

# Who I am

I am Adrienne Lynn Willis
I am the Lord's creation

I am His servant
I am His friend
I am His child
I am His beloved

I was created for His purposes
I was created for His glory

I love Him and He loves me
I am His and He is mine

I am Adrienne Lynn Willis
I am the Lord's creation

# Not Disappointed

Lord, You are not disappointed in me.
No matter how I may feel, I will always be Your beloved daughter.

You desire me and have pursued me.
More than anything You desire close fellowship with me.
The idea that You are disappointed in me is a lie.

You love me.
I am Your beloved daughter, in whom You are well pleased.

# The God of So Much

What is God the God of?
He is the God of many things.

He is the God of eternity
 The God of time

He is the God of heaven
 The God of the angels

He's the God of the universe
 The God of the Super-clusters
 The God of the Milky Way Galaxy
 The God of the Solar System
 The God of the sun
 The God of the planets orbiting the sun
 The God of the Earth
 The God of the moon

He is the God of the sky
　The God of day
　The God of night
　The God of light
　The God of the atmosphere
　The God of the clouds
　The God of the four winds
　The God of rain
　The God of thunder and lightning
　The God of mist and dew
　The God of snow and ice
　The God of the northern lights
　The God of rainbows

He is the God of water
　The God of the ocean
　The God of the seas
　The God of lakes
　The God of rivers
　The God of streams
　The God of pools

He is the God of the continents
　The God of Africa
　The God of Asia
　The God of Europe
　The God of North America
　The God of South America
　The God of Australia
　The God of Antarctica

He is the God of the biomes
  The God of deserts
  The God of mountains
  The God of valleys
  The God of forests
  The God of jungles
  The God of plains
  The God of grasslands
  The God of tundra
  The God of polar ice

He is the God of the four seasons
  The God of spring
  The God of summer
  The God of autumn
  The God of winter

He is the God of animals
  The God of mammals
  The God of reptiles
  The God of birds
  The God of amphibians
  The God of fish
  The God of insects

He is the God of people
  The God of men
  The God of women
  The God of adolescents
  The God of children
  The God of infants
  The God of the unborn

He is the God of the different races
  The God of the Aborigines
  The God of the Africans
  The God of the African Americans
  The God of the Asians
  The God of the Caucasians
  The God of the Indians
  The God of the Latinos
  The God of the Melanesians
  The God of the Micronesians
  The God of the Native Americans
  The God of the Polynesians

He is the God of families
  The God of husbands
  The God of wives
  The God of fathers
  The God of mothers
  The God of sons
  The God of daughters

He is the God of Love
  The God of Faith
  The God of Hope
  The God of Joy
  The God of Peace

He is the God of Wisdom
  The God of Knowledge
  The God of Understanding
  The God of Creativity

He is the God of Holiness
 The God of Righteousness
 The God of Faithfulness
 The God of Truth
 The God of Purity
 The God of Justice

He is the God of all of this and so much more.

# Part Three

# Pain

Nobody likes to think about pain, but it's a part of life and just because someone loves the Lord, it doesn't mean that they can avoid it. Everyone goes through times of struggle and doubt and I'm no exception.

I've been through a lot of struggles in my life and this section reflects them. *What is Black?*, *I Don't Understand*, and *Frustrated* were all written in 1990.

*Help me, Lord* and *Hurting* were all written back in 1996, when I was going through a very rough period of my life.

God is not only the God of the happy times, but of the rough ones as well. He is there through the joyous times and through the painful ones. Our test is if we cling to Him during those times.

# PAIN

# What is Black?

Dear Lord, what am I?
Am I a black person or just a person?
I have black blood in me, but I also have white and native American.
Why then does anyone who looks at me say that I am black?
Just what is 'black' anyway?

My skin isn't black, it's brown.
So why am I called black?
What am I to call myself?

Dear Lord, please tell me what I am.
Am I a black person or just a person?

I don't like to think of myself as black.
I prefer to think of myself as just me.

But when I say that do I really mean that?
Or do I just want to run away?
Am I trying to ignore my racial identity?

Is a black person supposed to like certain things?
Is he or she supposed to act in a certain way?
I don't know.
I wish I did.

Dear Lord, I've had many privileges,
Privileges that many blacks and whites haven't had.
And I feel guilty for having had them.

When I'm with blacks I feel out of place and guilty.
I'm usually more comfortable around whites,
But when I'm with them I feel out of place and guilty.

Dear Lord what am I?
And where do I belong?

# I don't Understand

Lord, I get so confused sometimes.

Today in Psychology class they were talking about death.

One of the lectures had known three people who had died young; friends of his who had been in an accident. One had only been eighteen, the others sixteen and thirteen.  Other classmates started talking about people they had known who had died young.

As I listened I got terrible depressed.

Why God?

Why do You allow it?

Why do so many people die young?

Why?

I love You, Lord and I trust You.

But there is so much that I don't understand.

# Frustrated

Lord, I get so frustrated sometimes.

It always seems that I'm either doing, saying, thinking or wanting
things that don't please You.

I love You, Lord and I really try to please You.
But I always seem to screw up.

All I really want is Your love, acceptance and approval.
I know that I'll always have Your love.
But I don't always feel that I have Your approval.

I know that You know the core of my being
And sometimes that terrifies me.
Maybe You know something about me that I don't
Maybe I don't really love You at all.

# Help me, Lord

Dearest Lord, help me.
I need Your mercy and I need Your love.

Storms are battering at my life.
Winds are tearing away at my faith.

So much threatens to tear my away from You.
For me, almost every moment is filled with fear.

Sometimes I want to see You so badly that I hurt inside.
I long to see Your face smiling at me with love.
I long to hear Your voice telling me that all will be well.
I long to feel Your arms around me and to know that I am safe.

Lord, I can't bear to live without You.
Without You there is no life.
Without You there is nothing but a dark void of emptiness.
Sometimes I feel like I am plunging into that void.

Lord, I need you.
Help me, please.

Be my tower and my defense.
Quiet the storms within me.

# Hurting

Lord I'm hurting

I'm frustrated.
I'm angry.
I'm afraid.

My friends have abandoned me.
I'm always the one who calls them.
And when I do they're either too busy or not there.
Nobody understands me.

Everybody wants to change me.
If something happens I'm always made to feel that it's my fault.

I've betrayed You, dear Lord.
I've ignored You.
I've broken every promise that I've ever made to You.
Sometimes I don't care.
Sometimes I wonder if You even exist at all.

I feel like a failure.
I have a terrible time seeing anything good about myself.
Even though I know You love me...
Deep down I don't believe it.

I'm afraid to live.
The whole world seems overwhelming and unfriendly.
I don't know what to do with my life.
I don't know myself.

I'm afraid to die.
Sometimes I'm afraid that if I die I'll be a failure in Your eyes.
Sometimes I'm afraid to die for fear that I'll find nothing.

# Part Four

# PSALMS

The Book of Psalms is one of my favorite books in the Bible. 'Psalm' means 'Song of praise' and the Bible is full of them.

But a psalm doesn't have to be in the Bible. Any poem or song written to God is a psalm and this section is full of my psalms to God.

The first psalm in this section is one of my earliest works, I wrote it around 1983. I was writing a story and in one part of it everyone was gathered at a worship service to sing. I tried to imagine what they were singing and *I Praise You, O God* was born.

Many Biblical psalms are prayers and so is the second psalm in this section. I wrote it while I was attending the University of Findlay. It was Thanksgiving break and it occurred to me that Thanksgiving was the time when we ought to be thankful for our blessings. So I decided to write *A Prayer of Thanksgiving*. I've made some editions to it over the years.

The rest of the psalms I wrote during my years at Messiah College. There was a period when I was very interested in the Biblical psalms and decided to try my hand at writing some in similar style. *Who is Like the Lord?* and *Trust in the Lord* are the results.

At the same time I also made Personal Translations of the already existing psalms 121, 124 and 130.

One of my favorite types of Biblical psalms were the creation psalms. I've always loved nature and God, to me, has always seemed the most powerful as the Creator. I decided to write a creation psalm and tried to make *Praise God For His Creation* a masterpiece.

When my nephew, Quentin, was born six years ago I promised myself that I would pray for him every day. *Prayer for my Nephew* is some of what I pray for.

*Prayer for my Unborn Niece* was made on Wednesday September 10, 2008 1:50 A.M., mere hours before my niece, Sydney, entered the world.

# PSALMS

# I Praise You, O God

I praise You, O God, Creator of the universe,
I praise You, O God, Lord of all there is.

You are above us all.
Your glory outshines the heavens.
You are the Ever Living, the All Knowing, the All Powerful

I praise You, O God, Creator of the universe,
I praise You, O God, Lord of all there is.

# A Prayer of Thanksgiving

Thanksgiving is the time to for looking back and being thankful.
And for all the blessings You have given me, Dear Lord, I thank You.

Thank You, Dear Lord, for giving me life.
 For giving me an immortal soul and spirit
 For giving me a healthy body
 For giving me an alert mind
 For giving me the ability to know right from wrong
 For giving me a heart that has always longed for You
For all these blessings, Dear Lord, I thank You.

Thank You, Dear Lord, for my relatives and friends.
 For giving me two parents
 For giving me three sisters
 For briefly giving me a brother
 For giving me a grandfather for fourteen years
 For giving me a grandmother for thirty one years
 For giving me a dog for twelve years
For all these blessings, Dear Lord, I thank You.

Thank You, Dear Lord, for my material blessings.
 For giving me a home
 For giving me an education
 For giving me food and clothes
 For giving me the opportunity to travel
For all these blessings, Dear Lord, I thank You.

Thank You, Dear Lord, for always being there when I needed You.
 For comforting me when I was sad
 For guiding me when I was confused
 For forgiving me when I sinned
For all these blessings, Dear Lord, I thank You.

Thank You, Dear Lord, for keeping me on the right track.
 For making me aware of when I had sinned
 For keeping me miserable until I repented
 For restoring me to right standing with You
For all these blessings, Dear Lord, I thank You.

Thank You, Dear Lord, for loving me.
 For dying for me
 For shedding Your blood for me
 For saving me from my sins
 For giving me eternal life
For all these blessings, Dear Lord, I thank You.

Thanksgiving is the time to for looking back and being thankful.
 And for all the blessings You have given me, Dear Lord, I thank You.

# Trust in the Lord

Trust in the Lord for He alone is worthy,
Trust, I say, in the Lord.

Men may brag about their strength,
But they are as unstable as water.

God alone is the solid Rock,
The One who will never fall.

His our refuge and our strength,
He is our glory and salvation.

Trust in the Lord for He alone is worthy,
Trust, I say, in the Lord.

# Personal Translations

Psalm 121

My help comes from the Lord, who made heaven and earth.
He is my Helper and my Guardian.
He never sleeps but watches over me always,
He will protect and love me forever.

Psalm 124

The Lord is my Helper.
Had it not been for Him I would have long ago fallen.
The Lord is always with me.
He protects me and keeps me from harm.

Psalm 130

I thank You, Dear Lord,
That You do not count the sins of those who love You.
If You did no one could stand in Your presence,
For You are holy and righteous.
But You are also loving and merciful,
And gladly forgive those who ask.
Wait on and hope in the Lord, all people everywhere.
For He shall redeem and save.

# Praise God for His Creation

Almighty GOD, You are the Creator of all things.
And I stand in awe of You.

All things were made by You, Lord God.
For Your purpose and pleasure were all things made.

In eternity past You created the realm of heaven.
A place unspeakable in its beauty.
A place where You humbled Yourself to dwell.
Although it could never fully contain You.

You created the multitudes of angels to be Your servants.
The Seraphim, the Cherubim, the archangels and countless others.
Magnificent beings like flames of fire.
All of them filled with glory and majesty.
All of which made the heavens resound with ceaseless praises to You.

You created the physical realm with all its wonders.
You formed this planet from nothing and shaped its corners.
You pushed back the darkness and caused the light to shine.
You created the sky and stretched it out like a blanket.

At your command the mighty oceans were made.
With a simple breath, You pushed them to their boundaries.
The waters foamed and roared and made way for the land.

You formed the dry land.
You carved the mountains, valleys and plains.

You covered the earth with soil,
And caused it to burst forth with life.
Out of the ground the grass sprang forth,
And covered the earth with a carpet of green.

Forests of trees sprang high.
From the mighty oak, to the great pine, to the slender elm.
All reaching up to the One who had made them,
All testifying of His power.
You scattered the land with flowers.
You covered the earth with a rainbow of color,
And perfumed the air with scents.

You formed the stars;
Procyon, Sirius, Alpha Centauri,
Epsilon Eridani, Tau Ceti, Arcturus.
You made the immense galaxies;
The Milky Way, the Magellanic Clouds,
The Triangulum and the Andromeda.
You placed the galaxies together in strings of clusters,
And stretched them throughout the blackness of space.

You created the majestic sun to give our world light and warmth.
You created the moon to light our nights.
You made the planets of our solar system.
Fiery Mercury, cloudy Venus, reddish Mars,
The asteroid belt, Mighty Jupiter, ringed Saturn,
Blue Uranus and Neptune, and icy Pluto.
You created them all and set them in their orbits.

You caused the waters of the earth to churn with life.
With a single word, You created the creatures of the sea.
The great whales, the fierce sharks, and playful dolphins.
The octopus, the squid, the sea serpents.
Eels, clams, starfish, sea horses, bass, flounder, trout and goldfish.
Marine life of every size and color swam in the oceans,
And filled the lakes, rivers and streams of Your creation.

You created the birds to soar in the heavens, roam the earth
and swim in the waters.
Eagles, hawks and condors.
Swans, geese, ducks and sea gulls.
Robins, blue jays, cardinals, crows and sparrows.
Ostriches, road runners and penguins.

Every sort of animal sprang forth from the earth at Your command.
The horses, zebras, gazelles to race the plains.
The deer, the rabbits, the wolves, to roam the woods.
The tigers and monkeys to prowl the jungle.
The mountain goats and cougars to roam the mountains.
The otters, alligators and seals to swim the waters.
The polar bears and reindeers to roam the tundra.
From the mightiest dinosaur to the tiniest insect, You created them all.

You created man, Your finest work, in Your image and likeness.
You formed him from the dust of the earth and breathed into
him the breath of life.
From out of the man's ribs you formed the first woman.
You brought them together and made them one.
You blessed them and made them rulers of all You had made.

Your work done, You looked over all of Your creation.
And You called it good.

All things were made by You, Lord God.
For Your purpose and pleasure were all things made.

Almighty God, You are the Creator of all things.
And I stand in awe of You!

# Prayer for my Nephew

Dear Lord I thank you for my nephew,
And for the great joy that he brings.

Please bless him and keep him safe.
Protect him from those who would harm him.
Let him never leave your sight.
Keep him always in the palm of your hand.

Shine down Your light upon him.
Bless him with ever more of you.

# Prayer for my unborn Niece

Lord, before you formed her in the womb, You knew her.
Now, before she comes forth from the womb, bless her.

Bless her and keep her,
Bless her and consecrate her,
Bless her and keep her always in Your care.

Let her be strong and healthy,
Let her have a heart for You.

*Wednesday September 10, 2008 1:50 A.M.*

# Part Five

# INSIGHTS

In addition to the Psalms, I also had a brief interest in the book of Proverbs.

While attending the University of Findlay I decided to try writing some of my own Insights.

# INSIGHTS

# God and the World

As the light of the sun is so much brighter than a lamp, so
    likewise shines the Lord.
He is the true light and He shines brighter than all the
    artificial lights that the world offers.

If one feasts on the Lord they will prosper, but if one feasts on
    the world, death results.

# Talents

Remember that your talents and possessions are gifts from the Lord. Never become proud because of them.

# Feeding

When you read a book you feed your mind.
When you read the Bible you feed your spirit.

You should be as eager to eat spiritually as you are to eat physically.

# How to Live

One's goal should be to live a life that pleases God.

Live your life in such a way so that when you die you have no regrets, and you know that you pleased God.

# Giving

It doesn't matter how large a gift is;
If it is given without love it is worthless in God's eyes.

It doesn't matter how small a gift is;
If it is given in love it is a priceless treasure in God's eyes.

Of all the things that we can give to God, the thing that
He desires most is our love.

# Hardship

Sometimes God allows us to suffer so that we can comfort
others who are suffering.
When you focus on God, your problems won't seem so big.

God created all there is.
He directs the stars and planets in their orbits.
He keeps the atoms of the universe together.
If He can do all that, then He's more than capable of looking after you.

# Love

A true Christian loves the Lord with all his/her heart,
And tries to put Him first in everything that they do.

Love is not just an emotion.
It is choice and action.

How can one say that they love the Lord and not obey Him?
How can one call him/herself a Christian and not love others?

# Rely only on the Lord

Don't judge the Lord as false because of the failings
of those who claim to follow Him.
Don't depend on institutions or leaders.

Man is fallible and will always let you down.
Only the Lord never fails.

Jesus Christ is the true Rock
Look only to Him.

# Being a Christian

Many people think that they are Christians because they belong
to a congregation.
Others think it's because they come from a Christian background.
Others think it's because they were born in a certain country.
Or because they believe in God and do good works.

It's not like that at all.

Being a Christian isn't belonging to a congregation.
It isn't walking down an aisle or being baptized.
It isn't just saying, "I believe in God."
It isn't even following the Ten Commandments and the Golden Rule.

Being a Christian means believing that Jesus Christ is who He said He is,
The Son of God and the only way to heaven.
It means making a total commitment to Jesus Christ.
It means making Him the Savior and Master of your life.

# Part Six:

# Essays

For this section I decided to compile essays that I have written over the years.

In 1983, when I was fourteen, I started taking a regular journal. At first I mostly wrote about trips that I took with my family. But started in 1984 I began to write my own thoughts and feelings in a series of essays. *Nature, Elements, Colors and Seasons* is one of them and one of my favorite works.

*What Truly Matters* was written back in 1990 and talks about what is important in life.

The *Tree of Life* was written during my time at Messiah while I was taking a Children's Literature Course. One of my assignments was to write a brief essay about an object of my choosing, but make it from the object's point of view and with a lot of imagery.

*Prince and Peanut* was written around the same time.

*My Room* was originally an assignment for a correspondence literature course I took after graduating from college. It describes one of my favorite places.

*Jordan* was my family's cocker spaniel for twelve wonderful years. He died on January 18, 2001 and I know that I'm going to love and miss him forever.

The Bible says that Christians should never be ashamed of Jesus and should always be ready to proclaim their faith. I am by nature shy and retiring, but *My Journey to Faith* tells how I became a Christian. *My Statement of Belief* tells what I believe.

# ESSAYS

# Nature, Elements, Colors and Seasons

*Nature*
I love nature, I always have and I always will.
There are several reasons and one of them is beauty.
In all forms of nature there is beauty, from the densest jungle
to the driest desert.

The Bible says that God's existence is proven by nature.
At first I didn't know what that meant, but I think I do now.
I think it means that when you look at nature you can see
the art and creation.
When you look at nature you can see careful balance and perfection.
You know that all this beauty can't 'just happen'.
Only God could shape and form it.

Nature is life pure, simple and wonderful.
Life itself is full of miracle.
From a tiny seed comes a giant tree.
From a small egg comes a living bird.

*Elements*
I love the elements; the sun, the wind, the rain and the snow.

The sun provides us with energy, warmth and light.

The rain provides us with water.
Water which gives life to all creatures.
Water which can make even a desert blossom with life.

The wind cools the world and carries the seeds and pods to new locations.

I don't know all the reasons for snow, but I do know that when it covers the ground and trees, it makes a scene of breathtaking beauty.

Each of the elements is so fantastic that only God could have thought of them.

*Colors*
I love nature's colors, especially green.
It looks beautiful in grass, leaves and plants.
The sight of a field of grass covering the ground with a blanket of green is one of the most beautiful sights that I've seen.
The sight of green covered trees dancing in the wind are truly sights to be thankful for.

Yellow is the sun, the ultimate powerhouse.
The giver of light, that gives life to so many.

Blue is the sky.
The great ceiling of the world.

White is the beautiful cotton puffs in the sky.
And the snow that covers the world in a blanket of beauty.

*Seasons*
I love the four seasons; spring, summer, autumn and winter.
I love the spring because it is the time of birth and renewal.
I love to see the flowers beginning to bloom.
I love to see the grass growing and new leaves budding.
Spring is the season of the birth of life.

I love the summer because it is the height of life.
The grass is greenest, the trees most majestic.
The flowers seem most beautiful and colors the most colorful.
Life itself seems to be at its fullest.

I have mixed feelings about autumn.
I live the cool, crisp feeling in the air.
I like the sight of the leaves in so many colors.
I love the explosion of red, orange, yellow and brown.
I do feel sad knowing that the leaves and plants will soon die.
But I know that the trees and plants are dropping seeds and pods
for next year's plants.

Winter makes me a little sad too.
It's cold, the trees are stark and all the leaves are dead.
But winter has its own unique beauty with its icicles and snow.
I also know that the seeds and pods for next year's plants are safely sleeping.
And that when the time comes they will awaken
When that happens, nature, the elements and the seasons
will again run their wonderful course.

# What Truly Matters

When I was young I often felt very small and unimportant.
At times it seemed that I was the ugliest and most insignificant
person in the world.

So I started having fantasies of wealth and power.
I would pretend I was physically stunning.
I would pretend I was a famous model or singer or actress or movie star.
The most beautiful woman in the world! My name in lights!
The idol of millions!
For a long time that was what I wanted most; beauty and fame.

But after awhile I learned that fame is fleeting.
New movies are made.
Different actors play the roles in plays.
New singers are constantly arising.
Beauty fades with age.
Fans find new idols and the star is in time abandoned and for forgotten.
If fame and recognition is ones goal, it's nothing but a futile fantasy.

In the end, what one does for the Lord is all that matters.
All accomplishments, if done for their own sakes, will crumble.
But if they are done for the Lord, even if man forgets them,
they will endure.

# Tree of Life

I am one of the trees of life.
I grow near the mighty River of Life that flows from throne of God.

Many people who have arrived from earth sit beneath my branches.
They sample my fruit and talk with others.
I love to listen as they discuss their lives in the earthly realm.
And how the Lord was with them through it all.

I especially love to hear the joyous multitudes sing and praise the Almighty.
Whenever I hear it, I raise my branches to the sky and I too praise my Creator.


Revelation 22:1-2

# Prince and Peanut

I've always loved dogs and I've known a lot in my life. Two of them were Prince and Peanut. They belonged to Mr. Yates, a neighbor of my Aunt Theda, who lived in West Virginia.

I don't know what breeds they were, but Peanut looked like a large black Irish Setter. Prince was a very large dog with a head that looked a bit like a German Shepherd, although his ears were flapped. He was mostly black, but had light yellow streaks on his legs undersides and face.

Both of them were outside dogs. I think the only time Mr. Yates ever allowed them inside the house was the time Prince was terrified of the 4th of July fireworks. Each of them had their own doghouse; Prince's was by Mr. Yates's house and Peanut's was across the yard by Aunt Theda's house. (Both Yates' and my aunt's houses were only a few yards apart from each other and they shared the same yard.

Mr. Yates kept both dogs chained in the yard, but they both had plenty of room to move around. Every morning he would unchain them and they would run up into the hills for awhile. He said that there was a creek in the woods that they would swim in. And I often wondered what sort of adventures they had when they were loose.

Right from the start I adored both dogs and I was always outside playing with them. For a long time I was especially fond of Prince. I was always petting him and saying "Good Princie-boy," over and over. Once, when I was about four or five, I crawled into his dog house with him. I remember him looking at me as if he was wondering what on earth I was doing in his house.

Mr. Yates often said that although Prince liked children, he didn't like most grown-ups. That made me worry that Prince wouldn't like me when I grew up. I could never imagine him being mean because he was always gentle with me and the other children who played with him.

Prince died when I was about ten or eleven, and Peanut became my new favorite. In some ways I became more attached to him than I had to Prince. Perhaps it was because I was older and knew that he wouldn't always be there.

Peanut died when I was in Junior High. I hadn't seen him in several years and was sad that I hadn't been able to say goodbye. I'll always remember him though.

Prince and Peanut...I'll always remember them both.

# My Room

When I was a little girl my favorite place to be was my room. It's changed several times since I was young, but for me the mood is still the same.

One thing I noticed very early about my room was that unlike the other three bedrooms in the house, mine was an almost perfect square. The guest/sewing room was square, but slightly elongated and my sister's room was rectangular. My mom and dad's room seemed gigantic. It was actually three rooms; the bedroom, bathroom and closet altogether. To me my room was the only one that seemed just right.

My room was also the most colorful. The guest room and most of my parents' room, didn't have any wallpaper, but was painted a pale green. My sister's room had smooth gray wallpaper and a green carpet.

When I was little the wallpaper in my room was yellowish brown and like woven thread in texture. The floor was covered with a mop-thick, bright yellow carpet. The window curtains were white and covered with red, orange, yellow and green flowers. My bed was a large single with white posts and usually covered with a bright orange spread.

On the wall at the head of my bed were two large pictures; one of Raggedy Ann and the other of Raggedy Andy. The figures had not been painted but sewn together from different pieces of cloth and placed on a bright white setting. They always greeted me with bright red smiles whenever I came in. With their fiery reddish orange hair and bright yellow outfits they seemed to light up the room.

Since they hadn't been painted and had no covering I could touch them whenever I wanted and I did constantly. I loved to sit on my bed and run my hands over them. I would trace their patterns with my fingers, touch their soft red buttons and Ann's frilly, white apron.

At the foot of my bed was a blue and white Raggedy Ann and Andy toy box/bench. My mom would sit on it while she did my hair. I loved to take things in and out of it and I would often climb into it myself.

Another unique thing about my room was my desk and clothes dresser. They were both connected and were part of the room itself, built into the walls. My desk was very long; it began a few inches from the head of my bed and ran all the way to the other wall where it turned right and connected to the dresser. I liked to run my hands over both of their smooth brown wood and I would often beat on them, pretending that they were my own set of drums.

Sometimes I would even climb on top of them and pretend that they were magic bridges or mountains. Other times I would crawl under my desk and pretend that it was a castle, or a fort, or a cave.

I also had a large walk in closet with a sliding door. Since it was the only part of my room that didn't have carpeting, that was were I would play with my blocks and puzzles. I also liked to play hide and seek behind my clothes, or close the door and pretend that I was a dragon in my cave. The closet was also were my book case was, so I would often go in there and read books on the cool floor.

I think one of the things that I loved the most about my room were its huge windows. One was right beside my bed and faced westward, overlooking our patio and the houses next door. From it I could also see a side of our house and could even see into my sister's room. Since the window was right beside my bed I would often sit (or stand) on my bed or sit on the window sill and look outside. I loved to look at the roofs of the other houses and up at the sky, especially in the evenings and at night.

I was a very imaginative little girl and I would often pretend that Peter Pan or some other magical being would fly through the window to visit me. On windy nights I liked to lie in bed, listen to the wind and watch the curtains dance. Sometimes I would pretend that the wind was calling me to dance with it and I would imagine leaping out the window and being carried away. I so loved to imagine that I could fly.

My other window faced in a northward direction and looked over our backyard and into the yards and fields beside and beyond it. I called it the Green Window because when you looked out of it during the spring and summer all you would see was green; green grass, green trees, green everywhere. I loved to look outside on stormy or windy days and just watch the trees swaying back and forth on the wind.

# Jordan

It was my sister's idea to get a dog. I'd always loved animals and wished that our family had a pet. But mom had made it quite clear that she didn't want the added responsibility.

Over the years I'd had a few fish and Jennifer had a turtle, a frog, a gerbil named Lisa and a guinea pig named Lady. But I'd pretty much settled on that being it.

Jennifer, however, had her heart set on getting a dog. And once she set her mind on something there wouldn't be any peace until she got it. For a long time she wanted a beagle. She even wrote an essay, "A Beagle for a Pet," that she gave to Mom.

Mom finally agreed to go look at some dogs and so, during the summer of 1989, she and Jennifer drove to the Petland by the Southgate Shopping Center. I was home from college and I went along as well. I personally thought we'd just look at the puppies and not actually buy one.

The store had a tan male cocker spaniel puppy in a display pen in the lobby. Jennifer had been going on and on about getting a beagle, but as soon as she saw that little cocker she decided she had to have him.

When we arrived at the store I wandered off from Mom and Jennifer to look at the different animals, so I missed the first meeting. When I came back over Jennifer was busy playing with the puppy and saying that this was the one she wanted.

To be honest I still didn't think that we'd actually buy him, but somewhat to my surprise, Mom made the purchase.

After the purchase the store put our new puppy in a box that said "I'm going home." on the side of it. The moment he was put into it he began to whine and fuss and scratch at the box, and did so the entire way home.

Jennifer was sitting in the front with mom and I was sitting in the back holding the box and getting a little panicked wondering what I'd do if he got out.

Finally, when we were getting ready to pull up into our driveway, he tore out a hole in the top of the box and poked his head out. As soon as he had his head out he was happy. Until we got inside he was a quiet as a mouse, just looking around at everything.

I had already thought that he was cute, but I think that was the exact moment when I first started to love him.

*Jordan - 1989-2001*
*Forever in our hearts*

# My Journey to Faith

My own journey to faith is a long complex one. Both of my parents had been raised in the church, but neither of them were churchgoing when I was young. Dad had had a bitter experience when he was young that forever soured him to religion and he had absolutely no interest in it.

Mom believed in God and enjoyed watching Robert Schuller on television. But she was a firm believer in 'to each his own.' She believed in God, but it was mixed with a hodgepodge of other things. For one thing she believed in reincarnation and she didn't believe in judgment. She also believed that all paths led to God and that as long as one followed the Golden Rule that was enough.

God must have had His hand on me because from the time I was little, I instinctively sought Him. Very early on I had a deep curiosity and hunger for things spiritual. I loved Bible stories and was very curious about God. On the few occasions my mom or some other relative took me to visit a church or Sunday school, I always felt a strange yearning. I wanted something, although I had no idea what it was I wanted.

Later I came to think of God as a big friendly person in the sky. Since I was very shy and had no real friends I came to think of Him as someone who I could talk too. But something was still missing and as I got older I started visiting different churches, searching for...something.

God must have given me some discernment. One of the first churches that I started attending regularly was a First Baptist Church. I thought the building was gorgeous (I still do) and I loved the music and the choir. But I still sensed that something was missing. The pastor talked about believing in God and following the Golden Rule, but that was pretty much it.

Right on my street there was a Unitarian church, but even though I had no idea what Unitarians believed, I never once felt the slightest inclination to attend their services. An associate of my mother's was a Jehovah's Witness and she gave me a Bible storybook. I loved the stories and the art, but I still sensed that it was leaving something out, although I didn't know what.

God also gave me protection. From the time I was 12 months old I was an avid book lover and, I read everything I could get my hands on. I loved to read about dinosaurs and prehistoric life and yet it didn't make me think that Bible stories were untrue. As fascinated as I was with science, part of me sensed somehow that Bible stories would lead me to whatever I was looking for.

I was fascinated with mythology. I loved Greek and Norse mythology, and was especially fascinated by the Egyptian gods. And yet I never once that that they had been real.

I was also fascinated with fairy tales and magic. When I was little one of my favorite shows was *Bewitched* and I was always wishing that I was a witch and could do such neat things. If *Harry Potter* had been written back then I would have wished that I could have attended Hogworts. And if I had ever found any books that taught how to cast spells I would have plunged right into them. But thankfully I never did.

I finally came to a saving knowledge of Jesus when I was between eleven and thirteen through a combination of reading Bible stories, gospel tracts and Christian comics.

Over the years Jesus has been about the only stable thing in my life and my closest friend. I love Him with all my heart and my heart's desire is to be with Him forever. He is my Lord, my Savior, my Bridegroom, my very life.

# My Statement of Belief

There exists one God Who has always been and will always be.
God is comprised of three distinct personalities; the Father,
the Word (Son) and the Holy Spirit.
All three are distinct and all three are one.

God created man in His own image to have fellowship with Him.
Man chose to disobey God and as a result fell into sin.

God is absolutely holy and cannot allow sin in His presence.
Because of our sin all of us are separated from God.
Since the punishment for sin is death, all of us deserve God's judgment.

Because of His love for us, God sent His Son, Jesus Christ, to earth.
Jesus, God the Son, lived a perfect sinless life.
He then died on the cross as the perfect sacrifice for our sins.
Three days later He arose from the dead.

Jesus returned to Heaven.
Someday He will return to judge and to rule the world.

Jesus' death and resurrection opened the way to heaven for us.
He gives eternal life to all who repent and believe in Him.